QUITE SIMPLY

poetry *Pt* today

QUITE SIMPLY

Edited by
Rebecca Mee

First published in Great Britain in 1999 by Poetry
Today, an imprint of
Penhaligon Page Ltd, Remus House, Coltsfoot Drive,
Peterborough. PE2 9JX

A Catalogue record for this book is available from the
British Library

ISBN 1 86226 538 0

Typesetting and layout, Penhaligon Page Ltd, England.
Printed and bound by Forward Press Ltd, England

Foreword

Quite Simply is a compilation of poetry, featuring some of our finest poets. This book gives an insight into the essence of modern living and deals with the reality of life today. We think we have created an anthology with a universal appeal.

There are many technical aspects to the writing of poetry and *Quite Simply* contains free verse and examples of more structured work from a wealth of talented poets.

Poetry is a coat of many colours. Today's poets write in a limitless array of styles: traditional rhyming poetry is as alive and kicking today as modern free verse. Language ranges from easily accessible to intricate and elusive.

Poems have a lot to offer in our fast-paced 'instant' world. Reading poems gives us an opportunity to sit back and explore ourselves and the world around us.

Contents

Memories

Different from each of us, city or country,
Children trying to be adults and vice versa.
When we sit and think of times long gone,
Forget the bad times, only recalling the good.
Unhappy childhood memories dismissed,
Cannot summon happy times because the brain hides!
Subconscious hides it in deep recesses.
So when I recollect my travels
I am glad of my writings in my diaries
And visit again the world in my words,
Pleased that the best is always close at hand.

Tilla B Smith

The Faithful Bear

(My bear during its life lost one of its legs which was replaced by a wooden one and a pair of crutches for support.)

Slightly battered, balding bear
Always so loved, always there
Since childhood you have stood the test
Giving me pleasure without rest
Listened in my times of strife
Helped me to find myself in life
Danced with me in happy times
Played your part in many mimes
Through our lives we've shared so much
You have always been my crutch
A part of my life you will always be
My faithful, wounded and battered Teddy

Christine Norton

The Shetland Massacre

I remember it well that terrible day,
The darkness the death, the water so grey,
All that we loved all that was free,
The life that was stifled, so inhumanly.

I stood at the cliff face, I took in the stench.
I imagined the smell of a world war one trench.
The disaster we all feared, it has now come upon us
The reactions of locals, the numbing of senses.

The coastline's black shroud, the sense of the dying,
The country has awoken, you can see people crying
This Russian roulette, is it simply a game.
Surely no accident, somebody's to blame.

Man yet again thinks he's so superior,
But when challenging nature, he ends up inferior
Man's trouble, pig headed, so stubborn, conceited,
He creates terminal death that cannot be defeated.

After hundreds of years you'd think man could see
Death and destruction - sheer stupidity,
In order to create a vision, a future,
Must rebuild the planet, help others to nurture

A world that is safer he must try to create
An awareness of pollution, he must try to debate
The preventing of coastlines from being destroyed
A new way of living, new methods employed

The cutting of corners, the saving of time,
Has created such havoc, a meaningless crime.
The disaster I witnessed and hoped never would be,
Was caused by an evil of wealth, greed and money.

What price the environment, the destruction we've wrought,
Think is it worth it - You may pause for thought

Simeon Nicholas Walker

Best Things In Life

There is a heady concoction
Of dry ice that smells of coconut
It chokes you but still you stand your ground
The lights and the heat mingle on your skin
With the goose bumps and sticky clothes
Sometimes security will douse you with water
And you smile as the mascara runs down your face
The vibration from the noise pounds in your chest, under your feet
Afterwards, you can't rid your ears of the ringing
There's the chat with the stranger next to you
Or the jostle of people at the back, craning
Then the magic comes
The silence breaks and the lights dim
You hold your breath and your heart stops
The band walk on stage

Deborah Counter

4

Together We Will Make It

You have been with me for a very long time.
The first time I saw you I knew you'd be mine.
You take me out of my depths of despair,
Whatever happens I know you'll be there.
You carry me off to places unknown,
More often that not - we are all alone.
I'll always treat you with great respect
I know, to rough handling you will object.
So far you have never let me down -
In the depths of the country or in the town,
And when I leave you - to wander at will
I know you'll be waiting for me still.
For I know I hold the key to your heart,
'Cause without it my friend you'll never start.
The love of my life you really are
My best friend and saviour my little *red car*.

Molly Tainton

That Picture In The Frame

It's only a picture in a frame,
It's more precious than silver or gold,
That picture tells a story of love, of life, and fame,
It's very old and beautiful
And not in a golden frame,
It's thirty years and more now,
And it always looks the same,
Each night as I look at that picture
I seem to hear it say,
Don't worry mother we're near you,
It's you that's far away,
When the dark nights come,
As they come to us all,
We must sure lean on faith,
And hope morning calls,
And I know as I look at that picture
That's so very special to me
With tears in my eyes, as I soothe all my sighs,
Thinking of years that's gone by,
Then I look again at that picture
And call them by their name,
I'll remember them forever,
No one else can be the same,
I'm proud of them in that picture
It's the treasure of my life
And I hope it lasts till memory ends
That picture in the 'Frame'.

Margaret Emsley Smyth

I Have Delicate China

I have delicate china
And glittering glass,
Silver ornaments,
Gold bangles and brooches,
Embroidered cloths
And fine paintings.
But my little candlestick
Is my favourite.

When we were young
And poor
He filled my heart
With rejoicing
Because he emptied his pockets
And bought me
This little candlestick
Made of brass.

My little candlestick has held many candles
But no flame has been as bright
As the love which gave it.

Bridget A Kane

7

Innocence Asleep

She sleeps the sleep of innocents: -
Her body, cresting the bed sheets in chaos,
A jigsaw of impossible beauty.
This room is her kingdom now.
This brittle bed her throne.
And I am exhilarated in her presence
And guilt-ridden in my voyeurism.

An innocent hand straddles my chest.
I dare not breathe -
Lest I startle the doe-eyed beauty
Into a forest of awakeness.
Each finger a playful child
With a mischievous mind and a tender heart.

Her breathing is regular and soothing
As the to-and-fro of the ocean,
Her bareness a landscape of ice-smooth ravines
My empire crumples beneath the trumpet of her laugh
My will dissolves against the crucible of her kiss.

Her hair meanders purposefully across my arm
Her gentle brow, an unsoiled beach
Before the muddy footprints of worry and of stress.
Lips smooth as clay, tongue a scarlet petal.
Each blinking eyelid,
An eclipse of a silent moon behind a cloud of lashes.

I have found pure innocence in an antiseptic world.
I just don't want to awaken it.

Andrew J Detheridge

Best Things In Life - Cheltenham Town A.F.C. In the Football League After 107 Years!

When the 'Robins' won the trophy
At Wembley twelve months ago
I thought 'This can't be bettered' -
The fates said; 'Oh, is that so?'
Consistency over the season
Was the key to success,
And beating Rushden on their own ground
Just couldn't fail to impress!
That Thursday night at Whaddon Road
Will live until my dying day;
Yeovil Town were the visitors -
A far better team when away!
Two goals in the first four minutes.
The play swayed to and fro,
Six thousand plus watchers held their breath -
Who would win? We didn't know!
In the sixth minute of added time
The ball found its way to Keith Knight,
He made a touchline-hugging run, then
Crossed from way out on the right;
Victory and Duff went up for it
But 'Duffer's' head got there first;
As the ball bulged in the back of the net
I thought the stand roof would burst!

The open top bus tour has taken place,
They came in from miles around;
The place of the Gold Cup and festivals
Has won even more renown;
The 'Boys with the tractors' have done us proud,
'Cheltenhamshire' and Cheltenham town!

Bill Pullen

First Choice

For me, life itself, is the very best thing,
It's a priceless gift that can't be compared
To material things, for which we covet and crave,
The world's a beautiful place with
Delightful things in it,
So, to get the best things in life,
May folk struggle and save.
I enjoy my life, the fresh air is free,
The sun's warm and bright, e'en the moon
Smiles down, at the dead of night.
Children's faces aglow, happy doing
Their 'life's best thing,'
Spreading joy all around with
Their laughter and fun.
I've had many blessings in life
For which I give thanks,
But to bring joy to the sad, and lonely
                                    ones too,
Is worth so much more, for it brings hope anew,
Sometimes fate takes a hand and we
Don like what we're given, but one of
The best things in life is the promise of Heaven.
The whole world is full of our sisters and brothers
Who need love, life's 'Best thing' above all the
                                    others.

May Dabrowiecki

Mystery

A warm feeling arises
in my centre
growing
invading my chest
moist
slowly floating
like fog
suddenly
rushing to my fingers and toes and cheeks
hot
an urge to flow
the fog condenses as it touches the air outside me
some tears sneak their way down
speechless
thoughtless
thankful
thankful
of this mystery
of existence
small and smaller
I am
not important
not at all
but still I am.

Thank you.

Mala Eggers

Grandchildren

Some are baby boys
Playing with brand new toys
Some are baby girls
With lots of lovely curls.

They are born into a world unknown
From danger and sadness are free
Innocent to harmful things
Just waiting for what mummy brings.

Grandchildren are a special gift
A treasure so lovely to hold
A lump in the throat at times they bring
When they grown up strong and bold.

They look to you for fun and advice
Bring proud sense of praise within the voice
Like a lovely meal which has a choice
When they are yours, their special and nice.

Our sons and daughters lived in our quarters
Their children are a special part of you
They learn to respect their nan and grandad
Hold you most dear like nan does her handbag.

There's something so lovely
When grandchildren visit you
It makes you feel bubbly
Although you must listen too.

My grandchildren are so special to me
Three of them for all to see
Liam, George and little Poppy
Grandad loves hem like he does his coffee.

P Harvey

Eighty-Eight Keys

Among my many treasured possessions there is one that I
favour more.
My Piano, with eighty-eight keys,
My new digital monster, with it's computer brain,
Playing this instrument, will never be the same.
I have been playing Piano, since I was four.
Many teachers failed dismally to teach me the notes, the
Crochets and quavers I was unable to learn.
Their respect for my natural ear, I could never earn.

I continued to play by ear, I joined a small band when in
my teens,
I sang a bit too, all the has-beens,
The old favourites, Gershwin and Porter they were the
tops.
Then in the forties it was all jiving and then came the
rock.

Now my fingers are getting old and tired, I caress the
Notes of my new Piano, which has been greatly admired.
I can record, and build up tracks,
Playing strings, trumpets, and even a sax.
I can enjoy the music of so many era's
As my mind wanders freely, to picture the times of long
ago.

No, I would not dream of parting with my Piano, that is a
comfort, and a friend,
My fingers will always caress the black and white keys
until the very end.

Helen Phillips

13

Best Things In Life

As I watch the beautiful sky
A delicate shade of turquoise
Speckled with clouds of navy blue
As the glorious sun is shining through
It makes me think of who put it there
And oh to breathe the wonderful air
For us all, He had a magical plan
He put us here in this beautiful land
With sea and mountains, lakes and streams
And all the changes of the Seasons
Then He gave us the eyes so that we
                              could see
The creation's beauty eternally
And with our ears we can hear the
                              birds sing
And with all He's bestowed on us, His
                              children.
He has also given us the gift
Of seeing the magic in everything.

Eileen Sheehy

Bret - I'll Stay Loyal And True

Bret - I put my pen to paper
And wrote this poem for you,
To let you know
You mean so much
And as a fan
I'll stay loyal and true.

Why are some people, like they are
All verbal and violent and sad,
They made a start
When they picked, on Bret Hart,
But he gave them,
      (What for) and I'm glad.

They can't take the pace
When he says to their face,
What he thinks,
And the words start to flow,
What he says makes me smile
Because he does it in style,
And his face has a radiant glow.

But only an idiot
Would put Bret down,
Can't they see him
For the man that he is,
Courageous and good,
'You know,' he's not made of wood,
So Applaud him,
      When he comes to your town.

Susan Elizabeth Senior

Shower Too Soon

Liniment and odd language . . . leather on wood . . .
Smiles and frowns . . . instructions to be understood.
Things become stifled: suffocatingly tense.
Words just bounce around the walls. . . making no sense.
Gumshields . . . shin pads . . . superstitions to perform . . .
Everything . . . anything to weather the storm.
Here's that grass laid out in a neat white square.
Man, you hardly notice, just to keep things fair.
Flags that flutter gently in the cold fresh air . . .
Voices that mist up the cold . . .cold eyes that stare.
Whistle, shrill and urgent, falls on your inner ear . . .
Yet another second in another year.
There's a tall burly voice that fills the air with 'Mine!'
And a little one behind claiming things are fine.
Speeding through the mire . . . three-quarter's murmurs mingle . . .
Squat-set . . . mouth dry . . . you sample that tackling tingle . . .
Stranded midfield . . . your hard shoulder glances and falls . . .
Sighs from the crowd at a tackle that appals..
Sour to the hour comes the taste of warm blood . . .
A weal on your lip in the churning mud . . .
The referee calls both captains for a little talk
And suggests the impossible that you have to walk!
So you're carried off for a shower too soon
On a rainy Saturday afternoon.

S J Shaw

The Party

The party would be like no other
They said. And they were right.
They sit together, Emma and her mother,
And ply their brittle chatter through the night.

But when the dark eyes find each other,
A challenge thrown as silent as a knife
Secretly they promise one another
Together you and I will fight for life

The daughter's secret nestles deep
Within the swaddling comfort of her womb
Kicking her heart with each prenatal leap
This tiny cameo of a world in bloom

The mother's secret too lies deep
Too deep for cure by drug or surgeon's knife
The swarming cells that bounds refuse to keep
Invading the last rampart of her life

And as she looks into her daughter's eyes
Admires the beauty she herself has grown
Young heart, young womb, does she there recognise
The awesome immortality we own?

Tom Owen

My Treasure

(Best things in life)

The best things in life are those I can see.
My sight is poor, so what I have
I value all the more.
I'm lucky I can hear and touch -
Enjoy mobility so much.
And I can see such super sights
That others might just take as rights.
Colours and clouds and sunsets, too,
Mountains and streams, a lovely view.
I find their beauty ever new.
And when the sunshine fills the skies
I thank my God that I have eyes
To see my family and friends,
Watch children grow and see their pleasure
In nature's wonders without measure.
Oh yes, there are no doubts for me.
My sight's my treasure.

P M Jay Smith

Stranger On The Shore

I met you then
So long ago
Two eras or three or more
In the bizzy, dizzy days of Mary Quant
When Trad-Jazz was the thing along with
                                the King.

You met me then
So long ago
Bought me a gift or two that Xmas time
Just as did the kings of old
You were my prince and we all know.
The gift of two was Jazz and you
Listening often
Loving them both
Music is the sound of love
Music is pain and covers every eventuality.

Gone now long, long ago
The jazz you bought which meant so much
                        - and you
My roses still rose, my thoughts still bloom
Though the slights still bruise in the same old way
Slightly touched by the tar-brush you'd thought
Subconscious speech with a song and a half for sure
And listening to your song all over again
As it pours across the waves of sound
Hear it truly all over again
            - Stranger on the Shore.

Renate Fekete

My Cat

The night is warm and quiet.
The sky hangs dark except for high above a tiny spark,
A starlit gleam to fascinate my eyes
While soft, so, soft a breeze quivers and sighs.

The perfumed blossom near
Floats in the air and petals lightly drift across my hair
Like nature's blessing, cool as the morning dew,
Refreshing, soothing, wafting its scent anew.

I stand and breathe the peace.
I do not speak, yet darker than the night a shadow sleek
Draws near. My outstretched hand greets fur.
I murmur then and hear an answering purr.

In secret ecstasy
A loving touch, a glimpse of glowing eyes which
Say so much and share my thoughts and then
Is gone .... leaving me to dream my dreams alone.

Catherine Clough

Faithful Favourites

When looking back at my favourite things,
There are so many that come to mind,
Some china, glass, bracelets and rings,
Music, books famous actors have signed.

But although I appreciate and admire them all,
The value is more sentimental,
My most precious favourite things I recall,
Are my dear pets, of course, preferential.

'Peppi' I had from a well known dog's home,
Was a mixture of collie and setter,
Her personality was one, second to none,
Loved all, and everyone loved her.

Henrietta, Silver Cloud and Motley,
Were my three fish of silver and gold,
Two molies named Dumpy and Portly
Were black, big eyed and bold.

The cockatiels, I'll never forget them,
My Timmy the first to my care,
Then Lucy, an orphan, a mate for him,
Her damaged wing a successful repair.

Timmy sang and danced at the table,
His Lucy he loved at his side,
His little heart broke when his lady,
Through illness, suddenly died.

All of my pets had adventures,
Of fun, excitement and spills,
I should write a book of their ventures,
In my poem there's no room to fill.

Monica D Buxton

The Athletic

Marmite sandwiches, glass of wine,
Curled up in bed with a magazine,
A fag in my hand
Listening to Van Morrison.
No phones, no bills, no ironing.
Pictures of my family in black and white.
Good news on the radio
Long lazy, leisurely sex
Without interruption, all is peaceful.
All my favourite things
The sound of the birds harping, gossiping in the
Morning, his sandwich box done and dusted
And me with a glass of wine,
Fag in hand
Listening to Van Morrison.

Air so blue with smoke and language,
Red with the blood of Cumry.
We articulate in our dissertations'
All who knew, played and worshipped heroes
Surround the sipping beer, cheering, incessant hub bub
'Get it organised club.'
Wales with might, slight, trite disguise
Plant the ball in England.
I look across at Dadi, nodding, grinning.

Men so loud and passionate,
Women, louder, more passionate
Finally meet half way planting their own balls
Displaying a wealth of love ingrown,
United at last in joy not born of curry sauce and chips.
In corners we declare undying love to peers
Full of tears we haven't seen in years, full
Of heraith of a country you accidentally forget.
I look across at Dadi, nodding, grinning.

I sip my bear and cheer . . . for Wales,
My favourite days of rugby and ugly men
Who will wallow in their triumph for days to come
While I allow in the arms of an English man
Wallowing in mine.
I will nod, grin, and think of my Wales.

Sharvn Davies

With Him In The Garden

(Dedicated to my old Christian friend
Sam Willetts, Philosopher, Engineer and Gardener)

Please do come in and look around,
Don't gaze too far ahead.
Take one step slowly at a time,
Gently be your tread.
Observe, take in, then breathe the air
Just listen, there's a presence there.
You ask me if my God is real
How can you prove the love you feel?
To fall in love is a personal thing
You wouldn't change it for a king,
And yet this being of all you sense
Removes ambition to present tense.
Growth and beauty is everywhere
It's yours to keep, it's natures ware
Silence is power the beauty is strength
In manifestation he goes to great length
For a glimpse of his kingdom just come in and look
Each scene is a painting from a heavenly book.
For a moment stop searching be at one with the scene,
You'll know you are standing where the master has been.

Peter said to Jesus, Master it is good for us to be here. Luke 9 v33

A Lucas

My Love

Dear one, I wish that I could spend
The rest of my life with you.
Just think of all the happy times,
And the joyous things we could do.

I would leave the house each day,
To toil at my daily tasks.
While you would stay at home for me,
What more could any man ask.

I would be with you in the morning,
And come home to you each night.
All day I would think only of you.
So fresh, so clean, so bright.

The sound of your voice enthrals me,
And when I'm sitting there with you.
I think of all the things you say,
That have meaning for just we two.

With you in my life at the weekends,
I would have no need to go out.
We'd spend every minute together,
That's what my life would be all about.

I wouldn't want you to be working,
While I was not at home.
I only want you to be there at night,
Just the two of us, just we alone.

My life would not be worth living,
If you were ever to go.
I'd tell everyone about my love,
For my hi-fi by Sanyo.

Ian W Archibald

Motorist's Delight

Oh! To be a motorist
In England's pleasant land
Getting clamped and all of that
Is really not too grand
Petrol prices rising high
On every budget day
Where is the money coming from
Is what most people say
Insurance charges rising high
Reaching up towards sky high
M.O.T.s and road tax
Parking charges too
Cameras by the roadside
Big brother watching you.
The poor old motorist's pocket
Is really not that deep
Some have wives and children
They really have to keep
Hammer the poor old motorist
Make him flavour of the day
Throw at him the bloody lot
To get from him your pay
Who would be motorist
In England's pleasant land
Where driving on our nightmare roads
Is really not that grand
Smog and fumes and traffic queues
They really are no joke
For every lady motorist
Or just your average bloke.

Eleanor Dunn

The Country Lover

I must rise in the morning when the sun is coming up
To walk through fields of daisies and smell the buttercups
To see the dairy cattle as they slowly chew the cud
And the beauty of the apple tress as they begin to bud.

To scramble through the bramble trees where the damsons will soon
grow
To walk between the hazel trees where the harvest's never low
To spy a weeping willow tree sighing in the wind
These are the real familiar things that I have left behind.

To rest against a silver birch next to a supply ash
To skirt around a blackthorn bush walking through it would be rash
To walk the headland of the meadow where the larks fly overhead
Those are the sights and memories locked forever in my head.

To spy a fiery stallion chase the mares across the field
To see a towering Oak close by who stands tall and will not yield
And his neighbour standing close to him the mighty chestnut tree
I am a country lover, in the country I am free.

When walking down a leafy lane, I see a robin with a worm
The seagulls screeching overhead as they herald in a storm
I listen to the music of the blackbird and the thrush
And see the fox cubs and the vixen dozing in the bush.

I hear the giggle of the geese chase a cat across the yard
And pheasants on the wing, just like on a Christmas card
See the peacock spread his tail as he proudly struts my way
Just a few of the wonderful things I have seen today.

Johnny Carroll

Barney Bear

Barney Bear sat in the suitcase, he hadn't been played with for years
The lady who owned him had locked him away in a cupboard way
                                                    under the stairs
He was covered in cobwebs, a terrible sight, his fur was all
                                        threadbare and torn
One eye was missing, his ear hanging off, the pads on his feet were
                                        all worn.
For the past twenty years, he'd lived in the dark, dormant for most of
                                        the time
He knew he'd been left there, abandoned, he knew he was well past
                                        his prime.
He remembered the day he first came to this house, for Ann the day
                                        she turned four,
He took pride of place then, and slept in her bed, she'd hugged him
                                        until he was sore.
But he didn't complain when she squeezed him so tight, he liked to
                                        be locked in embrace
But the cuddles depleted as Ann grew up, so he ended up in this
                                        suitcase.
So now he'd been dumped in the darkness, feeling lost, lonely,
                                        depressed,
One day he heard voices outside in the hall, it sounded just like his
                                        mistress.
'I've got just the thing to make baby 'sush,' came the voice from
                                        outside the door,
The cupboard door opened, a long stream of light, and he felt himself
                                        tugged at once more.
After all these years in the darkness, he blinked his one eye, it was
                                        true,
Ann was brushing him, dusting him off 'There I've kept him specially
                                        for you,'
She said to her new son, as he lay in his pram 'I've kept him all these
                                        long years,'
Barney felt useful and loved once again, as his single eye blinked,
                                        filled with tears.

The baby boy squeezed him and gurgled with glee, as Barney
                                    struggled for breath,
But he didn't mind if he held him too tight, didn't mind being
                                    cuddled to death.
To be out of the cupboard and cuddled once more, out of the
                                    shadows so deep,
He felt the grip slacken, now he could breathe, baby had fallen
                                    asleep.
So Barney lay quiet, not wishing to stir, till baby should waken -
                                    but first,
He closed his eye tightly and said all his prayers, he felt he was
                                    going to burst.
How he was happy, being wanted again, after all these years locked
                                    in the case,
He snuggled with baby, and sighed with content, as tears soaked one
                                    side of his face.

Ann Graham

My Teddy

You were bought as a present
That was thirty years ago,
You were a little teddy
With two shiny eyes
And a funny little nose.
You looked so cute
I just had to put you on show;
First you were on the sideboard
That was your home for a while,
Then you were put in the bedroom
And there you've stayed in style.
The years that's passed by
Have taken it's toll with you,
For you're a little worn and tatty
But still look so cute;
You're my favourite teddy.
Though I've got many more
I don't think I'll part with you,
You'll be here for evermore.
I'm getting older now
But still like lovely things,
But since you were my first teddy
I guess you'll most likely
Be here with me to the end.
After all, your teddy's
Your favourite thing,
They're so cute - cuddly
And they don't say anything,
Just have a silent grin
Where the mouth's sewn in.

R Warman

Thee I love

A Teddy Bear as old as me,
With patches of cotton on paws and knee.
Coloured pebbles, feathers, moss,
Ancient coins and candyfloss.
Smooth, silver sand beaches,
The calls of gulls,
Punch and Judy, deckchairs,
And boats with gaily painted hulls.
Books and libraries, museums too.
Fairground roundabouts,
The railway at Crewe.
The Tudor period, George Stephenson's 'Rocket'.
Flying Concorde,
Though hard on the pocket.
Canals and narrow boats,
Fields and woods,
The smell of rain and leather goods.
Colourful kites, peas straight from the pod,
Cups of tea, dear old Ken Dodd.
Autumn berries, cold, sharp days,
The call of the cuckoo, and going to plays.
The smell of polish, ocean swells.
The Animal Kingdom,
And baskets of shells.

Ellsie Russell

The Cedar Tree

It was perhaps the last time
That Alice would be able
To go out.

With each day she grew weaker,
There was less that she could do
With ease.

During our conversation in those last weeks
She had mentioned her need
To see the Cedar Tree.

We drove slowly, the day was fair.
She wore a faint smile
On her pale face.

Suddenly we saw it in the distance
Silhouetted against the sky.
Alice sat up in anticipation.

As we reached the place where it all began,
Tears trickled down her wrinkled cheeks.
She sighed.

We carried the tiny figure
And settled her beneath the tree.
This was her Birthday wish.

Annie Rawsthorne

The Field - A Childhood Memory

Indoors means rules to be obeyed - no chance to shout or sing
And endless chores to be performed, restricting everything.
Yet to escape into my world beyond the garden gates -
A tiny stream, rough stepping stones, and Paradise awaits!
'Mid grasses higher than my head, bloom flowers of varied hue
Meadowsweet, proud cowslips, milkmaids and daisies too
Buttercups, ground ivy, dog roses pink and white
And purple vetch on mossy banks where moles dig late at night.
Pungent garlic mustard, stinging nettles to avoid -
Lady's Slipper, sunshine bright to keep the bees employed.
I hear the skylarks singing as grasshoppers jump for joy
And I am drunk with happiness, no need for man-made toy!
I marvel at the waterfall down by the willow-tree,
And know that God surrounds me as I dance in ecstasy.

Eileen M Pratt

Free For All

Never was sweeter music heard
Piped from an apple tree,
Nor can words be found to match
Nuance's melody;

The trees had all its apples shed -
Leaves smothering the ground -
I ventured forth to look ahead,
No master to be found,

Under the mesh of twigs and branch
Intricately knit
I stood well rooted and entranced,
The vocalist still hid;

While poured out ripples of delight
On and on and on,
I took a breath and crossed the tree
Whence came the heavenly song;

Once turned could spot a weeny thing -
Dunn little featherball -
With heaving redbreast loud a-sing -
No tickets - Free for *all!*

Verena Ryecart

June Morning

From my kitchen window I can see
Pink roses rambling weaving winding.
Wandering and cascading through
The twisting branches of the apple tree.
The June wind plays rough
And almost with a touch of glee
Sends the small green apples so newly formed
And clinging precariously to the bough
Tumbling mercilessly
Scattering them untidily
Upon the ground.
Early morning and the only sounds
Are the cooing doves
And the reiterant cuckoo.
The magpies converse
Like noisy castanets
Machine gun-fire, a raucous morse code
Answering each other
From my cherry tree
To the sycamore across the road.
My cats yawn and stretch
Flexing their claws
Upon the wooden rustic fence.
A dog barks
And from the house next door
I hear the old man's feet
Shuffle down his concrete path
And another summer's day
Is at its beginning . . . .

Ruth Kennedy

My Furry Friend

Fast as lightning, quick as a flash.
She's in and out of all the trash.
Orange flashes, stripes of black.
In all cat skills, she never lacks.
That's TIKI my sneaky, sly little cat.
Wet pink nose, vivid amber eyes.
Always willing to chase the flies.
Ready to play, full of fun.
Then relaxing in the evening sun.
Patting my legs as I go up the stairs.
My clothes covered in multi-coloured hairs.
Balancing on fences, so sure on her paws.
Can even use them to open doors.
Sleek and shiny, agile and cool.
That crafty cat is no one's fool.
Hiding in shadows, out of sight.
Ready to spring, and then take flight.
There when I'm feeling sad and blue.
My friend that is always trusting and true.

Charlotte Pace (12)

Music

Sing me a song
And I'll smile you a smile
Tune me a tune
And I'll stay for a while
Rock me some rock
And I'll find the roll
Play me a ditty
And I'll bare my soul

Write me a lyric
That's fit for a king
Play me a shanty
And I'll learn to sing
Any style of music
And I'll play my part
For all types of music
Have a place in my heart

Daryl Tomlinson

Goldenhair

Daughter who was sweet and kind,
Where are you now?
The one who was of open mind.

Who's beauty was beyond compare,
Where is it now?
That waterfall of golden hair.

My heart is torn apart,
Who are you now?
Where can we start,

To heal the rift,
What are you now?
How could you, our love degrade!

All of life is gone,
You are reborn now,
Darkness hides the sun.

We shall nevermore see,
That waterfall of goldenhair,
Your waterfall of goldenhair.

Linda Bedford

My Music

My singers on CD's and tapes
Those beautiful tenor voices
Of Lanza, Domingo, Pavarotti
I have these lovely choices.

Oh those songs of yesteryear
Like the larks upon the wing
Listening to beautiful music
Then hear those voices ring.

It's Mario Lanza that I favour
The loveliest voice of them all
And then when he starts to sing
All the world he would enthral.

I listen to my CD's and tapes
Those voices so crystal clear
I'll never lend them to anyone
In my heart I hold them so dear.

So keep all your modern music
And singers that cannot sing
I'll listen to all my tenors
And the joy to me they bring.

David Brownley

Time For Rhyme

I have a favourite pastime, I like to sit alone,
Away from the television, and definitely the phone.
To type away on my computer, when I get the time,
And tell all who wants to listen, my feelings in rhyme.

Whether it's about our life today, and the human race,
Or to cheer someone up, and put a smile back on their face.
Something on the news that touches all our hearts,
Or a special tribute, when someone close departs.

Whatever the topic I choose, the satisfaction is immense,
To read it back afterwards, and it making sense.
I totally enjoy what I do, rhyming is so much fun,
It also gives the freedom of speech, to say what to anyone.

You can make people laugh, and smile from ear to ear,
You can warn them of problems, and what they should fear.
To tell someone you love them, or just to say thank you.
Poetry is great communication, there's so much you can do.

David Alan Kinch

Dom Chad

It's curved and sharply pointed,
she clings to it, real tight.
It blushes pink in places
When viewed from left or right.
Tucked within her garment,
No other there to see,
A secret hidden by her heart,
Carried constantly.
This fashion died-out long ago,
Yet in its realm will stay,
Companion, constant, to and fro
Embraced both night and day.
It didn't cost a penny
'Though more to her than gold,
Its presence there forever
Cushioned in each fold.
A token of requited love
A gift of pure esteem,
Gaze on it and ponder,
Was it just a dream?
No, here it is as always,
Her fingers stretch within,
Caress and gently fondle
The shape of Dom Chad's pin.

Shirley Sammout

Draughty Antics

I've done some really foolish things
Whilst spending time with you.
Stealing blooms, and wheelie-bins,
I've been the perfect fool.
I say, you're here just helping
To wash my fears away.
But in the end you'll tempt me
Toward mischievous play.
I've left you many times before
And I have been quite fine.
But events come pounding at my door,
And there you are inside.
Indeed, sometimes you've helped me.
At times, led me astray,
Hit-me so hard when I sleep,
I've struggled through the day.
I've always said, I'll end it
And make my senses clear,
But it's so hard, once I sit
Behind a cold-refreshing beer!

Caroline Sammout

Daniel O'Donnell

My current favourite singer is a young Irish Superstar
I love his singing so much that I go to all his Concerts, both near and
far.
So I have travelled all over Scotland and parts of England and Ireland
as well
I am a member of his Fan Club and he gives great value as his fans
can tell.
Two years ago seven coach loads of us went on his American Tour,
And he gave us hours of Quality Time on this trip, that's for sure.
Next week I am off to Dublin to join lots of folk I now know.
Then we'll all join his latest Tour in Canada, starting in Toronto.
Daniel O'Donnell loves to sing and he sings with such emotion
That he gives pleasure to so many and inspires such great devotion.
He has been compared to the late Jim Reeves though his unique style
is all his own
And he is a man of ambition and he knows just where he's goin'.
This quiet and unassuming young man from Kincasslagh, County
Donegal,
Call fill the Sydney Opera House and New York's Carnegie Hall.
When he walks on stage his presence is quite electrifying
He has the audience in his hands . . . sometimes laughing and often
crying.
Such a natural performer as he follows his routine
Singing and dancing around and waving to familiar faces he has
seen.
After Concerts he comes out again to meet with all the folk
He chats for three to four hours with them . . . he is that kind of
bloke.
On stage he's a polished performer, extremely professional,
Off stage he's just an ordinary guy who is everybody's pal.
He has sold over fourteen million albums and is in the Country
Charts regularly
Twelve thousand tickets were sold in one hour at Birmingham's NEC.
Like a One-Man Tourist Industry he has certainly put Donegal on the
map

He's secure and well-adjusted . . . this quietly confident young chap.
He holds an Open Day at home for the fans to meet him and his
family.
And they queue up in thousands for a wee chat and a cup of tea.
Each year we all go to the Festivals at Kincasslagh and Dungloe
To meet this super Superstar as we all love him so.

Mary Anne Scott

My Family

My family are the most important people to me
I ask myself, where would I be without my family?
It is a special comfort to be at home around my family,
Where I feel safe
Sometimes my family gets me down,
But I constantly remind myself,
To forgive and forget and stick together.
I'm proud of my family.
We have had many good times, and a few sad times
I always pray for a lot more happier times to come
We have all experienced so much together
We've lost loved ones, yet our family is still around.
As we welcome the new arrivals into our family.

Jahanara Khatun

The Only One

All I really need in my life is him.
His gentle touch, soft words,
Spoken with such meaning,
And a passion I could never comprehend.

In the quiet simplicity of our time,
Together, as one, ever changing entity,
He whispered deep into my heart,
And changed my world.

Take me into your beautiful existence,
Make me, need me, want me, love me.
You are an angel in my eyes.
Our paths were drawn side by side.

When I called out to you,
You were there for me in a way I really needed,
You gave me life in your arms,
Now let me give you your dreams.

Holli Moulson

Music In The Minster

My thanks are going to Bruce for seeing me once more
Inside the vaulted Minster, in the House of the Lord,
Listening to Mahler's music, and to others we adore,
Re-echoing, ascending to the ceiling, crashing chord.

Here for almost a thousand years they've stood and prayed;
Slowly the choirs, scarlet and white, passed through the screen
With heads bent low, no sound of shuffling feet was made,
Till their disembodied voices came back, heard but never seen.

The breaking of the Bread, and a little sipping of Wine -
The people meekly kneeling or rising before the altar;
Once crowded out by Law, they would so easily combine
The Authorised Version of the Bible and the Psalter.

Janet N Edwards

Best Things In Life

When I was a child
I loved to play with dolls
My favourite was my old
Rag doll which Mum had
Made for me. We had
Such fun my doll and me.

I took her simply
Everywhere. She was my
Favourite friend. At night
When I went to bed be
Sure I had my friend
We snuggled down between
The sheets and soon to
                    sleep we went.

We had such pleasure
In the garden, playing
Mums and Dads. I had a
Tea set which I was very
Proud. Thank you Mum
For my friend and all
The fun I had.

Gladys Bartley

The Yellow Shoes

In early fifties I was a young sailor
Passionately fond of fancy hair-cuts,
Fashionable clothes and matching
Expensive shoes. In Hong Kong
I had a pair hand-made with soft
Yellow-leather which fitted my feet
Perfectly and harmonised with my white
And cream tropical suits. It cost me dear
But every dollar was worth it.
The compliments I received
Kept my ego boosted and satisfied.

I never did part with those shoes!
Although I do not wear them much
Nowadays except during summer,
In fine weather, at outdoor parties.
When I give them a loving polish
The leather shimmers like gold
Bringing many romantic, nostalgic moments
Alive. They are creaseless and supple,
Light, balanced and strong as were made
On the day, by a master craftsman
On the other side of the world.
Alas the craftsman, his craft
And materials are no more!

The yellow shoes have a special
Place of pride on my shoe-rack.
They have outlasted my youth
And I am sure their beauty and grace
Will remain with me to the end.

Shafi Ahmed

Life's Simple Things

The things that matter the most,
Are the things we take for granted.
The care we're shown, the love we share,
Are the things that matter the most.
Yet, these few simple things
Are the best things in life,
The events we recall the most.
So many wonderful things in life,
We all aspire to gain as ours,
Let's hope love's forever maintained.

The best thing in life for me,
Is the natural world we live in.
The water and sun are beautiful things,
Such glory we can not surpass.
Everyone thinks food and friends,
As the best things in life.
The natural world we live in,
And love 'n' care we all possess,
Are the best things in life for me.

Elizabeth Cook

Watch

My dog 'Watch' was such by name and nature.
Although he was only small of stature;
He stayed near me through cold and heat
And will scavenge the bones from the table when I eat.
He rolled into a ball at the foot of my bed
At night while I slept I could only see his red head.
Devoted and loving always ready to protect
If ever a furtive look he would detect.
He understood my every move - he always knew,
Even in Church he would sit next to my pew,
Alas! My faithful friend left me at fourteen,
I cried incessantly - to think he would never again be seen,
But he was now old and his red hairs were turning grey.
And so I mourned and missed my dearest friend, but pray
That he is happy and at rest, and hope that we meet again some day.

Georgina Knight

Rain

Pitter patter, pitter patter, beating on the pain.
Pitter patter, pitter patter, heavy is the rain.
Puddles forming on the ground,
Plip plop, plip plop,
The fresh new sounds of

Rain falling from the clouds.

The sky grows darker
As heavy clouds roll in.
Crashing thunder, frightening lightning,
Making quite a din.

My window, blurred with streaks of streaming
                                        rain.
Pitter patter, pitter patter, still beating on the pane.

As the rain grows lighter,
The sky grows brighter,
Dark clouds roll away.

Rain gone . . . . until another day.

Julia Newton-Mercer

To Be One's Self

My favourite hope is to be.
To be one with the bird and the tree.
To do my own thing.
To have my own fling,
And at the end of the day to be me.

Organisms such as we,
Are part of the sky and the sea,
And it is grand
To be part of the land
Which produces the fruit and the tree.

My favourite thing is the earth
Especially the land of my birth,
The roots are there,
But the buds everywhere
The same sky covers its girth.

The world is becoming so small,
We feel we can speak to them all.
And it is quite true
There are now very few
We can't reach within our phone call.

And this is as it should be.
We do develop you see.
So you are well known
And I am well known
For what the Lord made us to be.

Stella Portas

Thank You Lord

Thank you Lord for the spring
And all the lovely flowers
The clouds that rush across the sky
That make the April showers.

Thank you for the birds that sing
The chorus in the dawn
And the sky blue mountains
For the mist to rest upon.

Thank you for the lakes
The rivers and the burns
And for the stream that rolls along
To make the mill wheels turn.

Thank you for the moon and stars
So distant yet so bright
Thank you for the nightingale
Singing sweetly in the night.

Thank you for the forest Lord
The orchard cherry trees
Thank you for the honey
The labour of the bees.

One more thing to thank you for
And that is for creation
And one more thing to ask you for
To grant us all salvation.

Patrick John Cunningham
1922 - 1991

Treacle

It was from a dog rescue we bought you,
Quite a fair distance away,
Picking you from the queue,
Was not difficult that day.

You were so small and fluffy,
All black with a few white hairs,
Which were situated on your tummy,
But they are no longer fair.

It was not so hard to give you a name,
But it had to be unique,
Not like all the same,
So we decided on Treak.

You got on well with Penny,
And even now you still do,
Together you look so funny,
Our special, lovely two.

In the garden you play-fight,
Or curl up by the fire,
You two look such a sight,
Even pulling your toy tyre.

Such a loving thing you are,
You know when I'm upset,
No matter where you are,
You come running - my wonderful pet.

You're my close and special friend,
Who means a great deal to me,
With you I want to spend,
The rest of eternity.

R Thompson-Lawrence

Homeland

To dwell upon a fragrance wafted
                by the gentle breeze,
Amongst the rolling hills and
                    azure seas.
Eclipsed by cotton tufts of fleece,
Crowning emerald kings of peace.
To steep amidst unblemished soil
And gaze in wonder at it all.

Eyes skyward focused on a
                seagull's spree,
Mapping out his course and destiny.
Scanning the earth from his aerial
                    view,
Impressed against the sky's
                midsummer hue.

Abundant heather dons the
                distant hills,
Encased in grass and golden
                daffodils.
Showers of daisies scattered at
                my naked feet,
Resplendent carpet laid out in the
                hazy heat.

To dwell upon this distant plane
Where I return to once again.
To step amidst unblemished soil
And gaze in wonder at it all.

   Inga Hass

I Wish

I wish I was a fish dear,
I wish I was a squid,
I wish I weren't a cat, though,
I wish bins had no lid.

I wish I wish I wasn't,
I wish I wish I was,
I wish, I wished that
I wish I wished that
I wished that I wished, and
I wish that I didn't.

I wish I weren't a fish, dear,
I wish I wasn't a squid,
I wish I was a cat, though,
I wish bins had a lid.

I wish I didn't wish I wasn't,
I wish I wished I was,
I wish, I wished that
I wished I didn't wish, and
I wish I wished that I did.

Pippa Moss

Resurrection

Across the early bay
Ships at anchor ride alone together unseen.
Unseeing in the mist,
Foghorns that mourn voices forever drowned
And ages deep
Fall one by one to silence.

The dawning's shadow splits
To let in dayshine on the spindrift,
And seawrack spider's webs float across my face
As gently as when years ago,
Though you only touched my cheek,
You took my heart.

And so, heartless now, I have no fear,
For still I feel the frisson
Of your fingers on my skin,
And I am brave again, and young.

Rising,
With the sap of filtered sunlight on my back,
Unstiffened, fresh and brightning,
I walk homeward
As the lightning day invades the morning;
Smiling.

Jim Rogerson

Temptation

An ecstatic feeling goes through me
From my head right down to my feet
Every time I think about
That cream cake I'm wanting to eat.
Shall I lick the cream off first?
Or nibble at the base?
Do I worry about the calories?
And leave it in its case.
'Eat me' it yells again and again
Lip smacking,
I'm yearning to taste
If one mouthful I get.
It will 'all' have to go
There's no way that any will waste.

Janette Harazny

Passionate About Plants

I am passionate about plants,
the radiant rose and other fragrant
flowers from my own precious plot
(which may one day be all I have to
nurture as I wish) and gracious
glimpses of cranes-bill, cow parsley
and clematis which furnish lanes and hedges
along those country walks.

Perennials have a poignancy
as nature strives for balance,
sending succulent shoots from
the over - wintered earth and merest
'dry twigs'. I have never seen rainforest
but I know trees which daily bring
enchantment, whether silver green
or revealing all their symmetry.

Plants provide a feast of food for
all the differing forms of life,
a magical array of visual
pleasure to tired hearts and minds,
a harvest of healing for human - kind,
saving lives and assuaging pain,
so, be passionate about plants
and tend and care for Mother Earth.

Monica Redhead

Life

Life that is given, should never be taken away by man,
Enjoy your life, when ever you can,
Life is a precious gift, and should never be thrown away,
Make the best of your life, each and every day,
Man has but a short time to live, it's said,
Never speak those words, 'I wish I were dead'
Many a word spoken in haste and jest, have come true,
When it happens, people think why? What shall I do?
Then think, of those words they have spoken in haste and jest,
I wish those words, I'd never had said,
Some people live life for the day and not tomorrow,
Life should be lived in happiness, and not sorrow,
Make each day of life, full of fun,
For tomorrow may never come,
Life is but a journey through time,
Never think of the bad times, you have left behind,
Life is full of secrets and mysteries yet untold,
Surprises in life yet, still unfold,
How long will life last, no one can tell,
But the best thing in this life, is life its self.

Allan Young

A Free And Simple Pleasure?

What I do to unwind? Well, I am what's know as, an avid collector,
I collect avids . . .
No, no, no, I collect everything, the weird, the wonderful, the strange
the oddities . . .

My latest collection may be strange somewhat, to you, but to me,
It's enchanting, and different, a free and simple pleasure?
And if you put your mind to it, you could do it too, collectively!

I collect, to help me relax, unwind, drops of water!
Yes, isn't it great? Isn't it grand? What a life!
Those tiny individual transparencies, so rare, so sought after . . .

I collect them all in a bucket, but only the best will I pick!
They're so beautiful, They're wildly wonderful, I love it, Them,
And everyday I travel to the coast and deposit them all, in the
Channel! (or the Atlantic!)

It really is one of the best things in my life
And I get one of the buckets carried for me, by the wife!

You might have seen us, at the beach, Sunday thru' to Saturday,
Sometimes the Isle of Wight, sometimes Ladram Bay . . .
But mostly Hayling Island where water is in short(ish) supply
Cos' twice a day the estuary always runs dry!

They call me crazy, I cannot think why;
They make me sad, so sad, I cry and I cry but my appetite's always
sated
And my drops of water are never dry and are always, always,
perfectly
weighted!

So I'll always see this collection thingy as a perfick way of unwinding,
tis for me;
It is the best thing and I'll carry on 'til all me buckets are used and
I've filled in the sea . . .!

Ron Matthews Jr

Golden October

January glistens all wrapped in a shroud
March dancing daffodils growing in crowds
April violets modest and sweet
May when the blossom falls at your feet
June is the month of roses for brides
February's moon sends lashing spring tides
July is midsummer when all's at it's best
November is weary and time for a rest
Tinsel at Christmas cannot compare
With a huge bunch of holly hanging
                              right there
Mellow September with fields of
                              ripe corn
This is the month when autumn is born
Mellow September so calming to see
But it's golden October for me.

June Greves

63

My Best Things I Care For My Dogs

To me the best things in my life are my Dogs, Naej and
Reven, they are the best things in life I have to care for,
Like precious stones they are to me, so faithful and
                                  lively they are.

From six weeks old to the present year of eleven years I
Had my loveable dogs. So loveable they are to me,
I care and love them both so dearly, to me they
Are the best thing in life to me I care for.

They protect me with grace and love for me like
I am a mother to them, I mother them, like they are
My children to me. I care and love them so great,
I love Naej and Reven with grace and love
                                 And gentle care.

They help keep me on the go, I try and not given in or
Lose my willpower to live, If I feel down, I just think
Of my darling dogs and how I would be letting them
                            Down if they lost me.

They help me to stay alive, they give me love with
Grace and care, it comes right from their heart
And soul, I know then that they are my best things
                            I have to care for in life.

Sharon Joy Wandless

My Garden

My garden in summer is a haven of delight,
when springtime labours prove their worth,
when brightest colours merge amid the green,
sculpting forms of textured shade,
that would put an artist to the test.

How large, how tall the trees have grown!
I watch the bees toil tirelessly, serving
the rose, that queen of garden flowers,
yet mindful of their duties everywhere.
The kindly sun illuminates my paradise so fair.

Shadows softly lengthen as the cool of evening comes,
with the garden at its loveliest, or so it seems to me.
Its muted shades are softened by the glow of coming night;
the white rose gleams mysteriously,
in purest, gentlest light.

Megan Guest

The Sense Of Touch

(Dedicated to Clare Maxwell-Hudson)

Back in ninety when my life
Had changed beyond compare
I embarked upon a massage course
To make me more aware
Of how wonderful the body is
No matter it's shape and size
Now it's underneath my fingertips
Where my future lies.

Calming people
When they're stressed
Soothing aches and pains
When using many different strokes
No two are the same.

Swedish massage, intermediate,
sports and M L D
Shiatsu, Facials, Reflex
and Aromatherapy.
they're courses run by C M H
Some intros, others whole,
I'm telling you they're all so good
They touch Mind, Body and Soul.

There's one more thing
That I must say
To make it fair and square
Thanks from my heart
Happy Birthday!
Cheers to the lovely Clare!

David M Carter

Bookends

They just look like two bookends,
Sitting at my feet,
One she wants to play all day,
The other just to sleep.

One's intelligent and fearless,
The other large and strong,
But anything you teach her,
Won't stay in her head long.

When I am relaxing,
And my mind is running free,
Two big slobbering wet dogs,
Will jump upon my knee!

When I take them walkies,
And throw for them a stick,
One of them comes charging back,
And knocks me down for six!

Their tails will wag in greeting,
They amuse me to no end,
They always run to meet me,
Because they're my best friends.

Jeffrey Kelly

An April Garden

Cool air freshened by a sunlit shower
Breeze carrying an earthy smell of life
Bright verdant growths of spring's unfolding leaves
Emerge from twigs, cropped by the pruner's knife

Neat soldiered rows of embryonic plants
Stand boldly in their livery of green
At smart attention to the solar rays
Black fertile aisles of new-tilled earth between

Pale and dark, in alternating bands
Lawn striped by whirring blades short clip
Edge embroidered, yellow, white and pink
Fat bumble bees, the nectar's sweetness sip

Beneath a sun-reflecting wooden fence
Sheltered from odd flurrying flakes of snow
Fresh shooting canes portent a prosperous year
Encouraged by the zealous gardener's hoe

Bare kitchen patch in Christmas garb re-dressed
Neo-frosted by the scattered lime
Awaits a final touch of grooming rake
New seedlings put to Nature's trust and time

Sharp cracking sound - a minor pistol shot?
Slow creeping snail falls foul of speckled thrush
Crisp shell, fragmented by the rockery stone
To feed a vibrant, rising lifestream rush

Ancient timbers on a weathered shed
Which stoutly stood the scathing winter blast
Now radiating April's growing warmth
Redolent of the garden's fruitful past

John Nolan

I See The Blossoms...

I see the blossoms on the Apple tree,
I see a skein of geese high above me
I see the moon, full and bright,
And stars that twinkle through the night.

Jenny flirts - but, scolding soon resume
Above the bee, that buzzes busily around a bloom,
The Thrush, repeating his dulcet trill
As the stream, murmurs past the mill.

The smell of bacon, cooking in the pan
And grass, as only new mown can,
Then bread, with new baked crust
Lift up my heart, and senses trust.

Those miracles do happen every day,
Thankfully, I kneel and pray,
They are *God* given, for all to see
The Best things in Life are wonderful - and free.

Frank Williams

Music Is My Favourite

What do we feel when we listen to music
There is so much inspiring our inner self
Do you find it better to just hear a classic
Music of Mozart or some jazz from the shelf.

In each tune there is a person alive
And in each line that person will strive
To fill our inner self with himself
As he thought and so spoke through each phrase.

Any orchestra is so full of sound,
Instruments are so full of melody
Altogether they are wondrous crowd.
They give us inspiration in mind and body.

John Roberts

To Feel, To Hear, To See

The richness of a Summer's day,
Peace and tranquillity,
My grandson's at play,
Nature's colour,
Birds singing, bringing in the new day,
A warm friendly smile,
Fresh water splashing onto my skin,
To feel, to hear, to see with wonder
All my favourite things.

C Parry

A Favourite Pastime

I like to sit and watch the sun
In its glorious splendour shining
And the trees above me with their branches
Spreading wide and high to shelter me
From the sweltering heat above,
And as I look up in the trees
Not a flutter of birds wings I see.
Only their chirping sound to be heard
To break the silence which seems to say
'Awake everyone and enjoy the sunshine
That makes the world so bright and gay.'

Sometimes I wish I was a bird
To soar way up to the sky
And when my wings get tired of flying
I can rest upon the sailing clouds.
But seeing that I am human
I am contented with my lot
To make do with the life I have
To walk and run and skip and jump
And thank God for making me
The way he wanted to.

Josephine F Welch

Flowing

I feel the buzz as I stride in,
Thinking oh yeah look at him,
I glance what do I see,
This huge thing next to me,
As I put on his tack,
Then I rise onto his back.
Give him a tap with my crop,
Off we go into a trot.
Wind flowing through my hair
What do I feel I don't care,
Galloping all the way,
On my huge bay.

Donna Carroll

Ginger

A little ball of a kitten
Smaller than a child's mitten
Lovingly accepted in our family
Unknown - whether a he or a she.

The male gender began to show
As our kitten began to grow
Fluffy and golden with long trails
Of tan stripes - to the tip of it's tail.

Inevitably - we named him Ginger
He was quite fussy about his dinner
Disliking cat food - was rather a bother
Yet lapping all 'leftovers' on offer.

Time to have our Tomcat doctored
Ginger decided to be very awkward,
Tiger capabilities, as he clawed the vet
Shocking transformation - of a loving pet.

His temper persisted for over a week
This dark side surfaced - a tiger streak,
Luckily - momentarily - short-lived
His continuous love - he would always give.

A handsome Tom - as large as can be
Yet his kitten-like ways - we would always see
Comical frolics inside our home - but outside
All roaming dogs would run and hide.

For seventeen years you remained by our side
Our saddened hearts - we cannot hide.
Laid lovingly to rest through our window to view
We shall always remember - and never forget you.

Norma Wales Lewis

Quiet Please . . . .

Fast, furious you serve an ace
Into a corner of my heart,
Passing my hopes with power, pace
To leave me standing, gasping, ripped apart.

Slow, anxious you hoist the ball high
Over the head to lob my mind,
Lifting my spirits with a sigh
To bounce, tormenting, teasing, close behind.

Fierce, frantic you return with fire
On a perfect line to my brain,
Clipping my dreams with desire
To land, embracing, chasing, once again.

Soft, gentle you guide a shot wide
Across the net to touch my soul,
Stroking my senses deep inside
To score, caressing, coaxing, with control.

Swift, ferocious you strike with skill
At the feet of my emotion,
Smashing my feelings with sheer will
To break, reeling, sealing, pure devotion.

Wild, excited you punch the air
To rouse, incite my obsession,
Courting my love with inspired flair
To win, inflaming, claiming my passion!

Susan M Billington

Xavier

The long wait is over, the telephone rings
She's gone into labour get ready to sing.

'It's a boy they tell me I cry with delight
They named him Xavier a prince so bright.

We look at him with loving looks that only
grandparents cannot miss, the smiles and hugs
kisses too that leave us with a glow.

We think his handsome and bright as button
our grandson Xavier we are so glad we have got
him.

Greta & Jeffrey Margolis

Skippy

I bought a little boy a handsome teddy bear
On which a notice said, 'I need much love and care'.
His furry legs could move, as did his arms and head;
The jersey that he wore was brightly coloured red.
I showed unto my wife this teddy I had bought.
'Oh, let him stay!' cried she, 'I just adore his sort.'
So then and there the youngster lost his brand new toy
And I had to go and buy another for the boy.
Now that explains just how our Skippy came to stay
And right into our hearts most swiftly won his way.
Just a lump of stuffing and two bright beady eyes?
You think that is our Skippy! Well, here's a big surprise!
He never looks the same. He's either glad or sad.
His conduct varies too. He's good but sometimes bad.
All day long he'll chatter to other household bears
Concerning what he's done, though no one really cares.
He thinks himself so clever, does our boastful Bruin;
His much inflated ego may bring him yet to ruin.
He's very keen on riding in our motor car,
Very proudly sitting up just like a movie star.
A stuffy toy may be but yet a friend indeed,
Who warm and loving comfort will give you in your need.
So here's to Skippy Bear and all others of his kind,
They're cosy when they're cuddled and all bring peace of mind.
So cherish well your Skippies; make sure you don't neglect
                                        them.
Remember, if they're tattered, yours is the love that
                              wrecked them.

C Champneys Burnham

77

Happy Days

I remember going to Orkney
On a great big boat
I hardly left the toilets
I was sick an awful lot.

We are on our way to Kirkwall
To start our holidays
And think of all the sights to see
What a lovely place to be.

We went to see the causeway
And the chapel made of scrap
Inside what a lovely sight
Everything was nice and bright.

Our holidays are over I am sorry to say
But the sights I have seen I remember today
We have to cross the sea once more
But I will be glad when we come to our own front door.

It's nice to sit down at our own fireside
With a biscuit and a nice cup of tea
Then I just close my eyes and see
All the places we enjoyed on Orkney.

Isobel Howitt

The Gardener's Dilemma

It's almost Spring, I'm really looking forward to the day,
When gardeners like me can start to set our seeds away,
We make the compost, fill the pots, and level off the bed,
And sow them very thinly, just as the packet said.

Excitement as the little darlings push up through the soil,
Tightly wound and tensioned springs, waiting to uncoil,
Tiny plants, unfurling, looking for the light,
As new born babies reach out for a bottle in the night.

We put them out, and bring them in, nurse them like a tot,
A little sun, and then some shade, whenever it's too hot,
We water them, and talk to them, as seed leaves start to sprout,
Proud as parents, giving birth, that's what it's all about.

We watch them very carefully, and pick off any bugs,
Inspecting them at dead of night to catch the snails and slugs,
There is one little problem, I'm puzzled, I must own,
It seems more plants have sprouted, than seeds that I had sown.

Still, never mind, it's best to have too many as too few,
I'll have to give some to my friends, and treat the neighbours too,
They're growing on, and now the first true leaves begin to show,
Once I space them out a bit, they'll really start to grow.

We separate them tenderly, and prick them out with care,
Although I've given some away, there's still a lot to spare,
The Gardener's Dilemma . . . impossible? . . . well nigh!
Deciding which of them shall live, and which of them shall die.

James R Storr

The Downs

I bring to mind the Downs in memory;
The scented herbs afoot towards the sea;
The Beacon view inland to iron age forts
And ancient man arising in my thoughts;
Chalk scars where man had quarried deep
In rounded hills where such men deeply sleep.
And in the war they ploughed the shallow soil
Which lay a thousand years untouched by human toil.
And I remember in a wood that nestled there
The bees had hung their nest, quite unaware
Of danger, from a bough across the ride,
And we would leave the track and round the side
'Till one day when we came, the nest was taken
And we were sad such beauty was forsaken.
And from that place low lying was a farm
Which adults viewed with some alarm:
I know it now as Charlston where the Bloomsbury set
Gambolled and painted as they met
Adding their colour to our lives,
Those complicated mistresses and wives.
And I return again and upward toil
To pluck a flinty arrowhead from the soil
And watch a hare cross wary o'er the bank
Where once the cowslips grew so rank.
I view this landscape made by nature and by man:
This priceless heritage for us to scan.
And treasure, for it lifts our spirits to the skies.
A panorama painted new at each sunrise.

Martin Knebel

The Best Things In Life

To trust and to be trusted,
Love given freely, by people who really care.
To be remembered kindly,
A gift beyond recall, is true love.
A healthy body and mind,
For little children to hold one's hand.
The time to sit and talk,
Money isn't any good to lonely people.
But someone who cares enough to listen, is!
A child's kiss and hug, and whisper,
'Nannie, I love you'
That's all that matters to some people
Time is the best thing in your life.
A smiling face, with a welcoming quip!
'Hullo, how are you today?'
Now maybe just maybe!
That is something to be remembered.
Many, many years afterwards.
Maybe a special Mother's Day -
Dancing for the first time for many years,
Meeting old friends, memories by us all,
Grandchildren, very much loved.
These are the best things in life!

Margaret Pearce

Anything Feline

Such beautiful creatures, all breeds of feline
The cat has always been a real favourite of mine
Wonderfully graceful but quick to move is the cat
Today they are man's best friend, I am sure of that

Cats like their comforts, love to be pampered at home
They know when they are well off, so far they won't roam
A nice sunny spot or your favourite armchair
Basking in heavenly delight, without even a care

Long wiry whiskers, sleek silky coats of fur
Usually so contented, they'll sit and just purr
Constantly just dozing, a ten minute catnap
They love to curl up in the warmth of your lap

Hours they'll spend washing and preening their coat
To look perfectly groomed for their owners to dote
During the day they're your companion and friend
To be cuddled and stroked, their time they will spend
They'll look at you smiling, the soft touch of a paw
They crave for affection, don't stop they want more

Lurking in the shrubbery, they anxiously await their prey
With back arched they pounce, not to let it slip away
So cruel is the cat, tormenting prey while it's alive
Much torture it suffers, it will never survive

With claws sunken in, the cat's finally caught the mouse
It'll then carry its trophy back home to the house
Cats like their own territory, they like their own way
Should an intruder invade, they are unlikely to stay

Cats are truly unique, with independence they're blessed
They make ideal pets, as friends they're the best
I will always love cats, they are a real favourite of mine
I just have never been able to resist, anything feline

Linda Brown

Our Darling

Ruff is getting on now; he has gone past ten
And maybe by the time that you are home again
He'll have found a Heaven where angels spend
Hours playing 'Ready' with doggies, on end.

But you mustn't think he's now a real old man.
He's the canine conception of Peter Pan.
He races around the garden like a two year old,
Understanding everything he is told.

At the same time each morning trembling he'll wait
For the sound as the paper boy bangs the gate.
With a bound he will snatch 'The Post' from the door
And shake it like mad, having fun galore.

To attract his attention from some such prank
We need only to say 'Ooo look, there's a Yank',
And straight away he'll leap on a chair from where he
Can satisfy his curiosity.

Craning his neck he'll grizzle and growse
'How dare an American walk past our house.'
But if ever American friends should call,
My goodness - the fuss that he makes of them all.
He fetches his ball, his bone and his shoe,
Ready to play and pretend they're you.

Joan Rea

83

Free Gifts Of Nature

The glistening white of driven snow.
A roaring fire with cheerful glow.
The chorus of birdsong every dawn
Greets my ears as I wake each morn.

Floating clouds in skies of blue.
Budding trees when winter's through.
Refreshing rain that kisses the land.
The restless waves wash golden sand.

Wild violets carpet the forest glade.
Ferns that flourish in damp dark shade.
Water tumbling down the hill,
A stream, a river, a sea to fill.

Wild heathers bloom on windswept moors.
A hunting hawk on the high breeze soars.
Singing frogs on a pond so calm.
The fragrant scent of lemon balm.

A host of bluebells 'neath twisted trees.
Cherry blossoms floating in the breeze.
A lark that's singing way up high.
Distant stars in a darkening sky.

Jagged rocks on a landscape wild.
A carefree smile on the face of a child.
Swans that down the river glide.
The beauty of our countryside.

Nature wonders all around.
So many treasures to be found.
Frost on cobwebs on winter nights.
Each season brings it own delights.

Pauline Coupland

Home Is Where The Heart Is

Home is where the heart is,
and mine, it is in Finzean,
with all its mills and purple hills,
The best to be brought up in.

David Duncan making spurtles,
Len, his Deeside Shortbread,
Clinter with its Auld meal mill,
and Stan his wooden buckets.

Peter Hill and Clochnaben,
stand still in all their gentry,
while Finzean School, it has some view,
The best in all the country.

Corsedardar monument standing tall,
Finzean stores down by the hall,
not to mention Finzean Church,
and lots of walks amidst the birch.

Farquharson Park and Sheltered Housing,
Even an Outdoor Centre.
Ian, the painter, Stan the Joiner,
and Tom our cabinet maker.

Finzean House in all its splendour,
Set amongst the trees.
But the South Drive is my favourite place,
It makes me feel at ease.

I love this place with all my heart,
It's beauty, I hold so dearly.
To me there is no place on earth
Like Finzean,
That's where my heart is.

Pat Lawson

Heroin Sleeper

6 am.
I get it as a treat
A 'Class A' gift
Something for the weekend
At the end of my travel,
I'd go far
But it got no further than the front room sofa,
With foil and a flame
Fried by my own hands
On nature's gift
A monkey for the inquisitive back
From a blossom of blood red
Into the blood of this blossom
Wilting,
In the dark of four walls
This wilting stem of wasted cycles
Blooming
With each nourishing inhale
It tastes foul and bitter
With a sometime caramel sweet draw
But, you forget that,
'A night-cap sir . . . can I interest you?'
Wrapped in cottonwool
With my insular glow.

Kevin Rolfe

My Pet Snuggles

I possess a panda in my flat
Its name is *Snuggles* . . .
I snuggle up to him in my bed on cold bleary nights
Snuggles has a pink heart shaped nose
With long droopy ears and mischievous eyes . . .
Snuggles watches me constantly as I potter around the flat
Between cooking and doing some embroidery . . .
My friends admire him and hug him sometimes
So that he too is a treasured friend like me,
When I sip coca-cola
I sense he smiles secretly on me.
My nieces and nephews
Enquire about snuggles from me,
I assure them that he keeps me from getting lonely
In the busy thoroughfare out there.
I won snuggles in a prize winning draw
In my area at work.
Snuggles is my bestest friend
I adore him lovingly . . .
I shall never part with him
As he is my precious jewel
In my crown . . .
Thank God for bears
They make life worth living . . .

Rita Cleary

My Best Things In Life

I find the best things in life, for me,
Are the simple things, like a beautiful tree
I love bluebell time, in a shady glen,
To go to a concert, now and again.
See a comedy show, and have a good
                      laugh.
When I'm tired and weary,
            a soak in the bath.
A good book to read, a laze in the sun.
Some friends to talk to, when work is done.
To see little children, eyes all agog,
To have a nice country walk and a
                drink at a pub.
See the beauty of flowers, in gardens
              around.
The flowering trees, all colours abound.
The colours of sunsets, on an evening walk.
Family around, with time to talk.
So many things keep coming to mind,
It makes you relax, and start to
              unwind.

Pat Rider

The Button Bag

The old brown bag with its brass clasp
Oh what memories are in your grasp
What does the bag contain I wonder
Why buttons of every shape and colour
What is this one we would ask
It's off an army coat it's brass
This one's off a wedding dress
Blue pan velvet what class
The pearl is off a matinee coat
And there's a hook off a fur coat
The clasp is off a bib and brace
And others we could never trace
There were buttons in two's three's and five's
Ready for use when the occasion arise
Belt buckles were stored with care
Some were round and some were square
There were other things in there too
A put and take, a bullet or two
Oh how many hours we spent picturing
With the help of my Aunt Lou
We were never bored by this little game
And I wish the kids today could find
The same pleasure in their grasp
As we did in the bag with the old brass clasp.

V J Bartrop

Ducks For Ever

Aren't ducks great?
They swim, they plod, they fly -
If only they had intelligence, too,
For who would walk
When they have wings?

They are my favourite thing,
More favourite than frogs or fish
Or even Pavlova - the raspberry kind.
They are so tidy,
Feather lying neatly on feather,
Pattern seemingly painted on
With a very steady hand.
And waterproof.

The ducklings are wonderful,
Fluffy scraps that can walk on water.
Windmilling their tiny feet,
Only the very young can walk on water.
The adults paddle calmly, except
In the spring when a young drake's fancy
Turns to thoughts.

Then one sees a rough courtship ritual,
As the drake almost drowns his chosen mate.
Drakes have no real subtlety, no finesse,
They are only after the one thing -

But aren't ducks great?

Ann Harrison

The Book

The book and I
Live this wondrous lie
Of pleasures that will never die.

Like two hearts that blend,
Like roads, that to the end
To a peaceful conclusion do wend.

My woes to share,
Faithful, full of care,
It comforts my soul which is bare.

Unobtrusive in my bag
To help me when I flag
Or when the hours to pass so drag.

Of outward shape so plain,
Within a host, a myriad drops like rain,
It soothes away the solitude, the pain.

This companion of my days . . . .
The book.

Frances Gillian Petroni

Beer

Suds they come in colours array,
Golden to brown, of Ales in cheer.
Be it red or even to say,
Black as Nuca's knockers.
And bodies vary,
To be drunk cool or warm,
Where potent may make a brewer's scorn.
Indeed there may be a housewife's displeasure,
From a trough to stream,
With a smaller measure.
Some chase with malt,
Or go for a pint 'n topper,
Until it's forty winks, when a drunken cropper.
And there's Snakebite,
To make you drown and totter.
With perhaps blackcurrant to flavour the grip;
When merry a gentleman may sing to his choir,
Until his world shall spin and tire.

Anthony Rosato

My Ted

I have a very precious bear
She goes with me most everywhere
Small enough for me to nurse
She lies concealed within my purse
Whenever I am sad or blue
I take her out and talk it through
She shows me all in black and white
So I will know what's wrong from right
I've had her many years I'm sure
A birthday present - I was four?
She's seen me through my tender years
And all my adolescent fears
Sat up with me on sleepness nights
Before exams and other frights
Through adult years we did not part
She saw me through each broken heart
A constant friend, a buffer zone
With her I'll never be alone
An omnipresent force it's true
Wherever I go, she goes too
And so you see my little bear
Is valuable beyond compare
No matter what woes or worldly strife,
'My little ted' a friend for life!

Ann B Rogers

The Cat's Christmas Tree

Observe the cat at Christmas time
How his eyes light up sublime;
The glittering Christmas tree
Is one gleaming tinsel sea.

With the baubles willing he mouses;
To him as safe as houses?
With them for days he plays
Or against them purring he rails.

Why do they sparkle bright
Like stars above the head at night?
A little jump and he can reach them
In a parade of skills quite solemn.

The tree's his world a-new.
His regimen has altered too;
Into a quite voracious scheme
Of sparkling lager and cream.

To stare and wonder's no disgrace;
Under the tree his life's in place.
New territory marked for his exclusive use
Safe from any dog's abuse.

Angus Richmond

Froggies

I have in my garden
A minuscule pond -
Not much to look at
But I'm very fond

Of the frogs who inhabit
This watery home -
Princes I'd scorn,
I prefer garden gnome!

At first I imported
Spawn from afar
But several years later
Fine froggies there are.

Tadpoles are cute
As they wriggle around.
Then several weeks later
Tiny froglets abound.

I do love my froggies
With jewel-bright eyes,
And long legs for leaping -
Is it any surprise

That I'm writing this poem
Amphibians to praise
And perhaps to help others
Fine froggies to raise?

Maria-Christina

The Stone

A stone, to be hand held.
Gathered on a beach miles away,
Smoothed by the forces of nature.
Painted by human hand.
A stone decorated by two pink tulips.
Of no earthly value.
Yet priceless to its owner.
A stone speaking of loneliness,
Of being locked in grief and despair.
Something to grasp to hold on to;
A reminder, that beauty still existed,
In her darkened world.
Its painted flowers spoke of gardens;
Of the Springs of childhood;
Of growth, of development, of hope.
The hard, unwielding rock,
Conveyed a sense of security,
Of solidarity, of contact
With the lost outside world.
Gazing at that stone,
She knew better days would return,
Light would flood again into her life,
She would recover.
The stone had been rolled away,
Her resurrection had begun.

Brenda Gill

Right Priorities

The emerald ring has gone
So has (Amongst dishevelled bedroom
Knickers and tights sprawled all over floor
And that)
The gold watch
The pearl necklace
The spangled earrings
The silver bracelet
All that weighed us down.

But, amongst the debris
Gibran's selected poems
Babaji's photograph
And picture with moon over water
Remain

The thief knew his prices
But not his values!!

John Crowe

Schoolboy's Favourite

Honey on bread is the sweetest thing
Bacon and eggs make the taste buds swing
Apple pie is fit for a king
But my favourite food is fudge
Yorkshire pud is what I like most
With my Sunday potatoes and roast
My sunniest breakfast is hot buttered toast
But my favourite food is fudge
Jam and cream scones are really a treat
Steak and onions my top choice in meat
Jam roly-poly a scrumptious sweet
But my favourite food is fudge.

G Carpenter

My Memories

I look to the future and what lies in store
I think of the past to what is no more
The clock ticks as time passes by
I try to remember but sometimes I cry
The best things in life are memories
And remembering how things used to be
My memories are like jewels that I keep inside my heart
Although sometimes they get tarnished from them I would never part
When I look through the pages of my memory
Into the mists of time
I see once again the life that was mine
I remember times both happy and sad
All the times both good and bad
I remember my dear old Mother and the way she cared for me
I know she wasn't perfect but she always tried to be
A memory to me is worth more than gold
A memory to keep to share and be told
I remember my childhood and of special toys
I remember friends both girls and boys
I remember so many things too many to name
All my memories are precious and all mean the same.

Christine Isaac

Best Things In Life Are Free

It's the little things in life that give me the
Greatest pleasure.
Their true value and depth I cannot measure.
I do know a smile, a nod and a wave of the
Hand makes my day seem brighter.
And cares and worries, disperse in the air and
My heart dances, refreshed and lighter.
I know the pleasure I derive when each morning
I open my curtains, as if for the very first time.
And I say out loud 'Good morning Planet earth.'
And I assimilate into my being God Great Spirits
Love and blessed sun shine.
My heart skips with joy, as I welcome each new day and
From my window I survey the surrounding countryside
My pleasure I just cannot hide, for I am happy and
Content, on my farm crouched in the hillside.
I gaze upon gentle sloping meadows and woods
Decked in their finery, of deep heavenly blue.
With gratitude my love and trust in God I pledge anew.
My favourite moments are watching the Mares and
Foals enjoying the Spring air.
And the sheep happily grazing, while their lambs frolic
Without a care.
I welcome the return of the house martins and swallows.
Best things in life are free, and I am here in my favourite
Spot with all the things I love around me, without my
Animals, the birds, woods, and flora, my life would be
Empty, and hollow.
It's the little things in life that give the greatest pleasure.
Not of ownership, or worldly possessions, but of nature's
Store of treasures.

Elizabeth M Crellin

My Teddy

I recall, snuggled in my own warm bed,
Holding tightly my favourite teddy,
My teddy was my companion, my love, my only love,
While I slept and dreamt, my teddy was there.

My teddy had a heart-shaped nose, with ruby red eyes,
My little Loveheart had a coat like the colour of the sun, the
Warmth of the sun.

I snuggle in my own warm bed,
Still holding tightly to my very favourite teddy,
My teddy still one of my companions, one of my loves,
While I sleep and dream, my teddy will always be there.

Angela Tsang

The Woodland Walk

Sitting here upon this bench
　　　Revives my tired soul,
It is autumn and the leaves lay golden
　　　Before me.
The trees are not yet skeletons but are
　　　Still partially clothed,
The birds here sing in freedom and call
　　　In all their glory.

Sitting here I hear the stream flowing
　　　Through to the sea,
I feel no tension here amongst mother
　　　Nature's growth,
I see the important things and they are
　　　Things I have and hold,
The material things in life are nice but
　　　What I see now is what I love.

Sitting here there is a stillness perhaps the same
　　　As a century before me.
The trees above and all around whisper in a
　　　Comforting tone,
Sometimes I want to stay forever to blend
　　　With the flowers and trees,
And to feel their peace as long as I live.

Tracey Ann Heard

My Piano

When life gets me down
With stresses and pain -
I play my piano -
Feel human again.

As I press each key
With soft gentle rhythm -
My body awakes -
And I sparkle within.

I transfer the music
Through both my hands -
My mind is at ease -
And I'm in command.

I play some Debussy
And maybe some Brahms -
The music gets louder -
Through both my arms.

If I'm in the mood
I'll play soft love tunes -
I'll romance the keys -
Like sweet honeymoons.

If I am stressed, then
Gerswhin is neat;
Followed by Mozart -
Chopin's a treat.

I look at my piano
And I'm really glad -
I practised my scales
When I was a lad.

My piano is my favourite thing.

Paul Ruthven-Lee

Buster

Buster is my dog
A Lakeland Terrier, fifteen today
His muzzle is grey now and his gait is slow
Once he was the busiest dog in the neighbourhood
No Postman, Milkman or Paper Boy was safe
He terrorised them all and yet he meant no harm
His energy knew no bounds but he would hurt no-one
Now he sleeps and watches me from the comfort of his bed
The Postman comes and goes unmolested
The papers not in shreds
My slippers now are all in one
And when at last his day is done
My heart will break - but we had fun.

Elizabeth M Marsden

104

Sunday Newspaper

I love my Sunday paper, the only one of the week.
No delivery here, no paper boy to tip.
A trip to the newsagent, driving mile after mile.
No thought for green lip service, for saving the planet and such.
My addiction must not be thwarted
No matter the state of the roads -
The weather, the chores, - priority rules.
Lunch finished as early as maybe,
Time to sit with the parts that I want.
Discarding the Sport and Appointments,
I settle, just me, with my paper, a cup of tea
A couple of hours and some music.
By the time evening comes and a play to watch on the box,
What better sport than the crossword
With Inspectors' Morse or Jack Frost?

Jean Greenall

Apt

You placed an 'oh' before my name
Before you placed your lips on mine
You held my face in your hands
While I held my breath
We could have had sex
You said I had great tits
We nearly had sex
Inside my head
You were inside of me
We almost had Sex, Sex, Sex
The way you touched me
We were just that away from it (click your fingers)
I felt your smile on my cheek
Almost
Nearly made it
Thank God
We made love
It's the best thing in life
Better than Sunset Beach
Even licks biting a ferret's tail
Surpasses Kate and Leonardo
Or rescuing Mudokans
Even better than chocolate?????
Even better than sex (liar)
It's two fire signs
Burning in the shafts of morning sunshine
You just can't help going into the light
It's so beautiful
When he fancies you
You fancy him too.

Jeanette Latta

My Constant Friend

Quaver is a special cat
I realised this when first we met.
She was chosen from a rescue home
Her coat was poor, I could feel the bone.
She had the most expressive eyes
And makes a horrendous noise when she cries.

Her colouring is a unique grey and gold
I adored the white spots on her chest and nose.
She is part Siamese and Burmese an odd mixture
In our home she soon became a permanent fixture.
Quaver's past a mystery will remain
Our love constant will remain the same.

She appeared to be fully grown
When distressed she will cry and moan.
Timid and shy she creeps around
Under the bed often she can be found.
Wonderful company and a personality
When spoken to, she will answer me.

In the garden to my surprise
She will run and jump after butterflies.
Our blackbird she will be aware
When it swoops down, it gives her a scare.
Now she is happy and full of fun
Up and down the stairs with her toy mouse she runs.
Quaver is now in the best of health
To me she is worth far more than wealth.

Aves Swanson

Altogether - Now

Lined up upon the rocks we stood,
De-briefing completed.
Both man and womanhood,
Some stood, some seated,
Waiting for our leader's last command,
That will take us to the joys
Of swimming unfettered, without band,
Both girls and boys.
'Ready all?' she calls, we take our bow:
'Then jump into the water, in the altogether - now.'

Reg Renwick

The Bullfinch

There is a blossom-tree I know,
And a pink bird, marked with black.
In the gardens where the cherries grow;
-Climbs the stem to watch the stack
Where he nests, and finds the hay
Warm and soft, and sweet, allway.
-Flies the garden; prompts the year
To recognise and prove him dear.
Summer comes, and he will know
The fruit - the leaf - the orchard lime,
That Empire calls in afterglow;
My Bird Book tells me that he's mine.
A black-cap he, and seldom heard:
Evening finds still sporting in the tree
Till late hours come and he's the bird
To vanish in a sun as pink as he.

                                    END

Robin Sackett

The Story Of Edward Cravatt

I'm a bear of impeccable breeding
From the very top drawer and all that
My pedigree goes back to President Teddy
My name is Edward Cravatt.

I have lived with one family only
Have been passed down from father to son
Each child had been coached on a code of bear practice
The result, my life has been fun.

At first I was just known as Edward
No commonplace Teddy for me
Then one of the family thought they would brighten
My life with a tie as you see.

Since then I've been Edward Cravatt and
It suits me right down to the ground
I think you'll agree that wherever you look
There is no smarter bear to be found.

Now I have a trustworthy young cousin
That my folks found on one of their tours
An aristocratic footballing bear
But not one of your terrace-type boors.

He is Archibald William Throgmorton
With stuffing as blue as can be
At last they have found a young bear of distinction
As a fitting companion for me.

Joe Silver

Chocoholic

A chocoholic? Yes, I am!
So keep your doughnuts stuffed with jam
Your macaroons and marzipan.
Your clotted cream and strawberry flan
Your custard tarts and peanut spread
Your brandy snaps and gingerbread
Your sandwiches and cheese baguettes
Your chewing gum and cigarettes.
Just give me chocolates by the score
And then some more and more and more!
Yes, I'm addicted to the stuff
And I can never get enough!
So keep your apples and your pears
Your oysters and your cream eclairs
Your bacon, burgers and baked beans
Your cauliflower and Spring greens.
A chocoholic? Yes, that's me
For I can't help myself you see!
So keep your noodles, curried rice
Your candied peel and sugar mice.
Your jellied veal and cottage cheese
Your Yorkshire pud and mushy peas
Your brisket, bacon, eggs and ham
Your pickled walnuts and your spam.
Your caviar and fresh French fries
Your scampi, crisps and your pork pies.
Give me Black Magic or Milk Tray
A Galaxy or Milky Way
But understand before I go
You'll never get my last Rollo!

J D Winchester

Wild Life In The Garden

The birds in the garden give me endless delight,
From very early morning until late at night.
'Bossy Beak' the blackbird is always first,
The others keep their distance, until he's eaten
                          and quenched his thirst.

Little 'Robin Redbreast' is braver than the rest,
He has a hungry partner waiting in their nest.
So he gathers up a large beakful of seeds,
Ever conscious of his partner and offspring's needs.

The greenfinches arrive in a great throng,
Much too busy quarrelling to sing me a song
All the others look on hopefully and really yearn
That there will be something left, when it's their turn.

I also have a family of grey squirrels to feed.
They climb up the Willow tree with such speed.
The peanuts they eat, and any they spill,
Are buried in the lawn, with such great skill.

A young dog fox has now joined the bunch,
He comes every day looking for his lunch.
I call him 'Freddie' and Flee our cat
Likes to curl up beside him, outside on the mat.

Many years ago having lived on a farm,
I am well aware they can lots of harm.
But I still hope, if the hunt comes this way,
He will live to delight me another day.

    Joyce Cambell

Sea Breezes On Summer Days

I sit on the beach
Lost in my own thoughts
Staring out at the large open sea
The pure blue water rushing up to the shore
I run my feet in the sand
It tickles in between my toes
I look up to the sky
It's a funny shade
With fluffy picturesque clouds
The warm sun beats down on my body
My skin feels warm to touch
The sun reaches down its long fingers
Over the calm sea.

Angela Couzens

Motor Dog

Here I am riding my bike
It's not a scooter nor a trike
I think a lot of my two wheels
It's rough and rugged and it appeals.
I can ride it on the road sand-pit or bog
I ride it on the road just me and my dog.
The dog sits at the back in her blue box
The wind blowing her ears and matted locks.
Everywhere we go people stop and stare
Look at that dog it's got some flare.
We ride in the sun wind and rain
I'll stop taking the dog when she complains
But when she stops waiting at the back door
We'll carry on biking as before.

James E Royle

114

Best Things In Life

As life progresses through the years,
Our ideals ebb and flow.
Our goals are changed as we mature,
And through our lives we go.
Best things for babies are at home,
Cocooned in love that grows.
A happy baby knows what's best,
And contentment clearly shows.
Best things for teens are lads and dance,
Disco music blasts the ears.
Career decisions to be made,
Boyfriends for the teenage years.
Best things in life for newly-weds,
Include a house that's new.
Building a home together,
With love so firm and true.
Time marches on, the children come,
They fill our lives with pleasure.
Grandchildren follow bringing joy,
To visit and to treasure.
Material wants may come and go,
But there's one thing that's true.
Best things in life are those love brings,
They last your whole life through.

M Baty

My Stuffed Toy

Tales of woe tales of joy
I can tell all to my stuffed toy.
His eyes do not flicker
Nor do we bicker.
Whenever I need a cuddle
His arms cling as my head's in a muddle.
And he lets me play with his long fur
When my eyes can't see from tears in a blur.
He's sometimes flung across the room
But that does not bring him to gloom.
For hours he just sits alone
While I am busy on the phone.
Yet when I enter the room
His smile is for me and it's not too soon.
The object of my affection
I could leave it to the reader's detection.
But it's a furry long haired orang utang ape
And he's really my best mate.
No walkies nor food to cook,
Nor do I have to read him a book.
Just sit him upon my shelf
That's all he needs for his good health.

Jean Rendell

Ode To Alf
(Dedicated to Alison Moyet)

Your voice washes over my mind,
With your words ringing sweet and refined,
You manage to soar,
To the elevated floor,
Where you leave all the others behind.
You dance with the stars the moon and the sun,
And the comets and planets they all look on.
You win me over with your power and strength
And you warm my nights with your poetic breath.
You take me to places only Gods have seen,
And you carry me upwards to the far extreme,
And as I weep as I hear you sing,
There's that feeling inside that you always bring.

David Simpson

My Favourite Things

I have two very favourite things
In fact they are a pair,
They sit upon my wall-unit
Watching o'er me in my chair,
It is two little fluffy dogs
They are so cute and sweet
And been admired so many times
By friends when 'ere we meet.
Who have offered to buy them from me.
But always I say 'No'
I'll cherish them and keep them close
Till the time when I must go,
They were a Birthday present
From my son - some years ago
I guess I'm sentimental - old fashioned- or whatever
But I wouldn't part from them
They're mine to keep forever.

Olive May Godfrey

Objects of Vertu

The Tobacco Jar

Capsule of rich aroma and mellow flake,
Cool the moist leaf within.

The Pipe Rack

Pine repository of fine briars,
Sombre reveries' sole companions.

The Crystal Bell

Light refracting, sweetly ringing,
Recollecting last farewell.

The Paperweight

Encased in glass, without expression
Tudor lady, who art thou?
Steadfast witness of my fate.

Portrait of T. as a Babe in Arms

Outlined in light; held in adoration,
Face turned towards the lens:
The focus of love,
The cause of delight.
An earnest of hope
The presence of life

.......and at two years.

Bronze hair; fair complexion
Promise of proud distinction
Sweet face, sad expression
Where's the grief? Wherein's the sorrow?
The heart to prayer to guard the morrow.

The Cheddleton Station Souvenir Mug

He wandered there midst the bric-a-brac of a bygone age,
Whilst we, becalmed in the blazing sun, wondered.

Gathering Faggots (After the oil painting by G Wood dated 1892)

Bowed beneath the heavy bundle,
Face chapped by December's icy blast,
Mindful of the coming snowstorm,
She quits the hoary heath
And turns at last for home.

Scarborough (After the etching by W L Wyllie R.A.)

Sea wash on sweeping shore,
Fishermen prepare to trawl the tide
Was it there in summer sunshine
We strolled arm in arm so long ago?

The Wizard (After the Royal Doulton Porcelain figurine)

Tall and spare, his gown
A swirl of spectral hue,
He appears deep in thought,
Hand upon the open page
Tracing the spell; the ingredients,
Freshly gathered
Pouched about his waist.
Silently he glides, intent upon the incantation
And vanishing, the very air is stilled.

The Silver Trinket Box

Grief's gift in fond remembrance
Cold glint, of triumph's steely stare'
Scornful pride, in satin's silven sheen.
There stands the casket
Death's victim, ne'er saw the sword,
Nor e'en the flashing spear
Vanquished, decayed, consumed, unmourned.

Malcolm G Cooper

A Special Box

Container of my inmost thoughts
This wooden chest contains the book,
The letters and the secret notes
Upon which no-one else may look.
And another box I prize,
A thing in Art's and Beauty's vein
Of sparkling jewels and deeply carved
With symbols of the most arcane -
Let it not be Pandora's kind
Which, from the tree of knowledge made,
Caused our hearts to grow so cold
Yet where hope remains our aid.
Neither let it be the Ark
Where within stone tablets lay.
Our spirit is in our living hearts,
Our thoughts within our minds to stay.
I have made this kist for you
Yet you, I would have rather kissed -
This polished box and close-fit lid
Yet I'd prefer a closer tryst,
A meeting of those precious things
That, in your special box, you keep.
Would I contain your love as much
Kept safe within a realm as deep.

Robin Kiel

Books Are Treasures

Looking at our bookshelves in all their disarray,
I get to contemplating, 'Must tidy them today'
It really takes some discipline, as I begin to stack
Each book in place upon the shelf, I don't *want* to put it back.
There's something interesting will always catch my eye
And then I find I'm reading. I realise with a sigh,
It really is a hopeless task and time consuming too
But even when they're tidied there are those I *must* look through.
So they are left just sticking out, reminding when there's time,
There's something jolly good to read, be it soppy or sublime!

Anything at times will do, 'Rupert Bear' or 'Winnie the Pooh'
'Herbal Potions' (Medical), Stories of God's Miracles,
Massive books about the Law, Winston Churchill's 'The Great War'
Also Earthly History, book on Bible Prophecy,
Loads of Christian Literature, and the 'Wonder World of Nature',
'Alice in Wonderland' I knew, (I wonder, what *did* Katy do?)
The endless 'Readers Digest' range, Classic Volumes for a change,
Always in mind is brother Jim, for many books belonged to him.
I haven't yet read 'Will' Shakespeare or got around to the 'Cookery
                                                        Year'
'Roman Britain'. I can't put down 'The Schooldays of Thomas Brown'
L N Alcott's 'Little Women', 'Good Wives' and 'Little Men'.
Interesting 'Birds of the World', 'Mighty Ships' with sails unfurled.
The 'Flying Scotsman' (Chariots of Fire). To see the film was my
                                                        desire!
I liked Science Fiction stories, Yes. I revelled in those 'glories'
Veterinary Tales (James Herriot) (Can't tell everything we've got!)
Languages - I'll *never* learn! (It's getting late, I must adjourn)
Oh! Many Bibles, old and new, Books of poems, we have a few
While *The Life OF Christ In Art'* I know with *that* I'll *never* part.
But I wonder why it seems to be, that I'm not keen on poetry?

Hilda Barrett

123

Awakening Thoughts

Sunrise over an azure sky;
The cuckoo's springtime cry,
Hedgerows garlanded with the blossoms
                     of May;
Hapless lambs gambolling -
Heeding not the time o day;
Young fledglings learning how to fly
                and swoop with ease;
Church bells proclaiming the
                worshippers pleas;
Sweet sleep;
Another dawn -
And chance to see and share the beauty
                of God's world.

Dorothy Sheard

Peru . . . .

A little hint of mortality moved me to travel before it was too late.
I journeyed South to meet a childhood dream: Peru.
A jewel sitting there, waiting for me. The apex of that
Lovely land: Machu Pitchu. I sat under the lone tree on
That high plateau and looked into Death's eye and gave it
the finger!

Jackie Callow

The Man!

Nearly 2000 years ago, an interesting report
Was written by a roman to an Emperor in his court.
Sent by Publius Lentulus, to the Emperor Tiberious,
Impressed by Jesus as a man, his *description* given
serious!
For every *detail* noting, having spoken with, and met
with our Lord Jesus face to face, he never would forget,
Today the ancient manuscript is still preserved in Rome
A letter which portrays *the* man, the *greatest* ever
known!
A copy of this letter, hangs framed upon my wall,
And now I'll share its contents with those not known
at all.
The copy that I printed is now a prized possession,
The words of which I have arranged in poetical succession
Therefore, my friends *read on, enjoy* a graphical description
That one man sent *another*, before Christ's crucifixion!
For *I* would not have read it, had not a churchman
thought
To print it in the magazine that Seaton Church had
wrought!

A man of stature, comely, tall, of *virtue* has appeared!
His disciples name him *'Son of God'*, as a prophet *most*
revered!
Among his *Gentile* followers, while all in need of healing
He cures, restores, makes *whole* again, these *miracles*
revealing!
His hair of *chestnut* colouring, curls and waves to *shoulder*
length,
And is parted in the *centre*, while his *face* shows beauty,
strength!
His beard is short and *forked*, and is the colour of his hair
His eyes are grey, - quick to *perceive*, in *reproving*
you they *scare!*

126

In conversation pleasant, *fair* in comment, gentle *too*,
Of body *excellently* proportioned, hands expressing
all to you!
Very few have seen him *laugh*, yet many have seen him
weep!
His words expressed with gravity, show feelings that
run *deep*!
A man *exquisite* - beautiful, in speaking, temperate,
wise!
So ends in brief, this one report, which comes as
no surprise!

Marcia Elizabeth Jenkin

Untitled

I thought it was a crime to cry,
But needn't have felt any sorrow,
We did not say goodbye,
So we shall have another tomorrow.

Lynda Cosgrove

My Life Enriched By Love Of Poetry

I am not rich, just working class
I enriched my daily life by poetry
I may never bring me monetary value to my door
As now and then I write my lines of poetry more
My words in poem, unfold my whole past life
The good times, the sad times, also my strife
Some of joyest love, some of failed love
That has happened to me through all my life
Some of how I was inspired by word or song
Or off all my emotions, as the years rolled along
Fifty-nine years I have seen go swiftly by
As if they were on wings of a butterfly
Some years brought my many tears
Also some brought me many awful fears
As I am now I can truthfully say
I survived them one and all my way
My greatest wish of all my life
Was to have true love at the end of my life
Alone I am now without my true love dove
Why have I been passed by left alone as one
Loads of love rages within my body, my soul
I feel now that I am doomed to be alone to grow old
I shall keep on praying that love will come soon
So I can end my loveless life, dearly loved - anew
I know one person loves me no matter what I do
That is you Lord in Heaven who created me also all of you
For His purpose which I cannot now see but one day He may
Convey His purpose to me, where in His home loved and cherished
I know I shall always be beloved by He, His helps me along when
Things go wrong. As I end this sad poem to you all, I shall go on
Trodding along searching for that true love, to end my old years life
With. Till my Love above in Heaven calls me to come to my new
World and His Home.
To be at peace with love surrounding my whole frail body
Forever eternally.

Bertha Shuttleworth

129

Severely Taken In

We have taken our traditional break, this year it's Spain and no
mistake.
Arriving early by aeroplane of course, we did the journey half the
time, last year by sea we crossed
Our hotel is not a grand one but decidedly plain but very clean, the
Rooms are light and airy the view surpasses dreams
Our balcony opens on to a plain blank brick wall as they are
building another hotel next door
They sincerely hope there will then be lots of tourists and the cash
Will roll in as they hope to extend more and more will the beauty
then blend?
Unfortunately we could not be moved as there were no other
vacancies forthcoming
The sea was some distance away we could hear Spanish guitars
strumming
We doze at random perhaps this spot will eventually be admired by
all
There is nothing that one may do except sunbathe by the hotel
pool

The hotelier is a friendly sort of man but insists we stick strictly to
his rules
He locks the main entrance at ten o'clock each night he is afraid of
drunken fools
This tiny village is so sedate and all appear petrified when you
approach they run away to hide
If it were not for the hourly bell tolling I should have thought all had
upped and died
We make the best of our remaining days the food has been plain but
wholesome
All Spanish cuisine of course some most inedible as I tried tempted to
eat some
We shall all leave with better figures as so corpulent we came
We are tanned and look delightful unfortunately there were no
postcards at hand
It does seem that nature forgot this place and threw away the key it
will of course blossom and be put on the map eventually.

All is so quiet and peaceful except for those bells and animals that
Abound and are continually chewing on the luscious grass that
                                        abounds
The bells they ring so freely like they have done for centuries old
I now think they are singing a fond farewell as slowly the toll grows
                                        cold
The hotel creaks and the rafters sag and the heat comes penetrating
                                        down
Although it's picturesque they have attempted to do their best what
                                        does the future hold?
Like a ghost town with no one around it seems to hold on to a fear
Our dilapidated coach awaits minus its clutch and brakes let's get
                                        away from here
The throbbing engine is revved up and splutters as we board
The driver speaks only Spanish with a dialect

Ronald Dennis Hiscoke

Classic Cliffhangers

Back in the hazy 60's
A series with classic cliffhangers and mysteries.
A police box overcast by a shadow.
A dalek rising from the Thames
A snake like device homes in on the Dr.
Time is treacle on reaching the Tardis.
The Dr and Jo hear something coming.
The Dr is pushed into a peladon pit
K1 advances on the unconscious Dr.
Nyssa says 'The watcher was the Dr all the time.'
Tegan laughs as a skull bursts out of a crystal ball.
Peri and Hugo watch the dome explode.
Mel screams as Andrews is electrocuted.
Mel is dinner for the OAPs.
The Dr and Ace walk off in the sunset
'Where to now Ace?'
'Home'
'Home?'
'The Tardis.'
'It was on the planet Skaro. . .'
As the next chapter has a go.
Over thirty years of time and space.
And in the curse of Fatal Death, many a face
Charted as the highest brand
With the Dr always on hand.

Theta Sigma

France 33 v Wales 34
'Heaven Sent'

Everybody told me -
That Wales were going to lose,
I told them that Wales would win,
They said 'What, you said who?'

'It's not likely that in Paris,
Wales will ever beat France,
For if they played in Britain -
They'd stand a better chance!'

But somehow, something tells me,
That Wales will win the day,
And I don't care who will laugh at me,
And I don't care what they say!

No one has ever listened,
To my feelings of Welsh pride,
They think I should forget about it -
And throw it to one side!

But my feelings for Welsh rugby,
Will never be content,
Until Wales play, like they did today,
A gift that's 'Heaven Sent'.

Bronwen Davies

Monkee Magic

When I think back on a sunny
day, I remember the Monkees
in a special way.
I think back to when I was a
little girl, when they seemed to
be my whole world,
Micky was always funny
Davy was so sweet
Mike was always steady
but it was for Peter my heart
was ready.
Those memories I will always
treasure, may Monkee magic
live forever.

Michelle Treacher

A Smile, Then A Tear

The aroma of apricot stones warming
Lured us to our beds.
It's going to be cold this night
Was what my Grandma said.

She tied the stones in pillowcases
Placed them at the bottom of our bed
She tucked us in warm blankets
Smiled and kissed our cold foreheads.

She said good night, I love you
Thank you for your thoughts this day
It's time for you to go to sleep
She then tiptoed silently away.

A fond memory of time gone by
A smile, then a tear
One of the best things in life,
Remembering my Grandmother's good cheer.

Gene Perkins

The Megastar Eros

I arrive at 'Le Club' in my stretch limousine.
At the door are the bouncers.
All handsome and mean.
The streets are awash with the fans and the press.
My limousine chauffeur assures me I don't look a mess.

I emerge from the limo.
A true megastar blow a kiss to the fans.
Whoever they are.
I stop to pose for a photo a minute.
The fans are all screaming they want to be in the photos.
Once inside I sip rum and coke.
Being with many friends near by.
I kiss many people close to myself.
But it's purely platonic as I mingle around then I seize my chance I
                                    must ask someone for a dance.
For a good night out.
I chat to Madonna who's sipping iced tea.
But others look on.
And she can't keep her eyes off me.
By looking so attractive man I am on the floor.
She is coming towards me . . . I must stay close and cool . . . then
                                    everyone shot, look she is talking to hi.
Who is him.
And wonder what they are talking about.

And so the Springtime.
We stand among the crowds of Piccadilly.
And their cheap affection.
Eros watching the corrupt city.
And through white eyes.
As the sun drags helplessly away.
And the city floods sensitive with evening colour.
Advertising endlessly its own den.

Externally oblivious to the loveless.
Mesmeric among the carcinogenic.
Eros flights his tome arrows.
Among the Piccadilly crowds.
As we stand in the lilac night.
Hand in hand as the theatres let us in.
The mystical and the unfaithful.
From the storm of sentimental arrow.
In the springtime city sky.

V Borer